More advance praise for *Go*

T0862294

Samiya Bashir's *Gospel* builds a vibrant, ascending num of wisdom around us, chronicling the life blood at the root of its making. Her poetic vision is limber and sensual, thriving amidst histories, love lessons and traditions at once singular and collective. To say, as she does, "I am not a fool who believes in things which hurt me," is to be lyrically aware of what sustains her, from mythic messengers to the ever-present legacy of queer black family: poets and kin all. It is to know that understanding survival is work and joy; one must invent bold images and sly rhythms to shape that play. This is just the kind of poet Samiya Bashir is: attentive, passionate, artful. With each line, her *Gospel* urges us to seek a like power in ourselves, and share it

—Tisa Bryant, author of *Unexplained Presence*

Samiya is as fine a poet as they come
As the title states *Gospel* is a song
It is beautifully crafted, touching and wonderful to watch it shake
shimmy
and move.

—Pamela Sneed, poet, playwright

If a volume of poetry can be a page-turner, *Gospel* is it. An ambitious storyteller, Samiya Bashir has created a four-part volume that grabs you and won't let go. Her poetry is urgent and feverish, mournful, sexy and healing. The only thing better than reading Bashir's words, so luscious and ripe you can taste them, is hearing her perform them.

—Linda Villarosa, author of *Passing for Black*

gospel

oems

gospel
oems

samiya bashir

✺REDBONE PRESS

WASHINGTON, DC
www.redbonepress.com

RedBone Press
P.O. Box 15571
Washington, DC 20003

ISBN 978-0-9786251-7-7
Printed in the U.S.A.

Cover photograph © Samiya Bashir
Cover design by Eunice Corbin
Author photo © 2009 by Wura-Natasha Ogunji

www.redbonepress.com

About the book

Gospel is an ecumenical resistance song in four parts. We enter at the crossroads, tripped up by trickster deity Eshu-Elegba. A chorus of crows, led by Norse god Odin's raven messengers Hugin & Munin, guides us into each movement. In this passionate follow-up to 2005's Lambda Literary Award finalist, *Where the Apple Falls*, Bashir's poems challenge truth to stare down the power of fear and paralysis.

"We intended gospel to strike a happy medium for the down-trodden," said gospel music pioneer Thomas Dorsey. "This music lifted people out of the muck and mire of poverty and loneliness, of being broke, and gave them some kind of hope anyway. Make it anything but good news, it ceases to be gospel."

The good news, according to Bashir, is that we are neither alone in our mess, nor alone in our grasp of the tools to heal. In this pull-no-punches collection Bashir lays down a road map, a portable flashlight, and a shaky-legged escort to usher the way toward recovered sight and strength.

Other books by Samiya Bashir

Where the Apple Falls

Best Black Women's Erotica 2
(editor)

*Role Call: A Generational Anthology of Social & Political
Black Literature & Art*
(co-editor with Tony Medina and Quraysh Ali Lansana)

Teasing Crow
(limited edition chapbook)

American Visa
(limited edition chapbook)

Wearing Shorts on the First Day of Spring
(limited edition chapbook)

For my grandmother,
Gwendolyn Russell Hilliard,
who insists on the importance of good news.

Acknowledgments

I am indebted to Fire & Ink, Cave Canem, The Austin Project, Soul Mountain, allgo, Alma de Mujer (a project of the Indigenous Women's Network), Astraea Foundation, the James Dick Foundation for the Performing Arts, RedBone Press and the many friends, family, colleagues and the universal posse of love whose support was integral to the completion of this book.

Grateful acknowledgment is made to the editors of the following journals and anthologies in which some of the poems herein originally appeared, occasionally in slightly different form:

Best Lesbian Poetry '08
Cake
Callaloo
Cave Canem 10x10
Queer Codex: Rooted
Queer Collection
Other Countries: Voices Rising
Reverie
The November 3rd Club
Torch
War Diaries

My village has three waterfalls three churches but no priest
The last one went off after a crow that cawed in Aramaic

—Vénus Khoury-Ghata

Contents

At the crossroads

We argue as if Capulet or Montague.
On neither red nor blue can we agree.

There is kicking. It hardly matters whose foot
starts the dance. Running and tripping

over path strewn rocks (how stupid we become
at these times) peering back to track any small gain

of the other. Cleavers clang their noisy impotence
against our steel trap eyes. Dare we slow down,

narrow our lids to see the laughing trickster
in his two-toned cap? Could it possibly matter

any less now? Against a moldy stack of uncashed
promissory notes, both borrower and lender

stand broke as you speak through my lips and cry
with my eyes. Funny how when blindness is contagion

light leaks in from our wavery source. There—
the piercing of our congruent laugh. To any twisted thing

we'll cling: these red dusted roads outside of Santa Fe,
my broken arm, those drunken Washtenaw streams, or that

birthday party where you climbed the emerald ash and showed
the world your underpants; that hot summer we swore we couldn't fall.

Hugin & Munin speak the scene

"Molten rime smelts
our April fool's destiny.
Learn ye well her well."

Now rise up, and get you over the brook

We've been reduced
to ice cold water, salt and
well-beaten rocks, as though

these old customs could possibly
sustain or keep us clean now. In truth,
we hardly remember these early folkways.

Ah, but what we have hidden – *glory!* – the angle
of dawn on our fingertips, pressed against our mish-mash
flesh. Your honeysweet lips upon mine at the first conscious breath.

First beer drunk & shot clock ticking

too easy to say it started on tuesday night.
average. work/school night. family hour to prime
time. digesting broadcast news rancid as discount meat.

how did we get here? on this rent-to-own couch,
greasy-fingered and scowl-faced. cussing out somebody's
children. belt worn to the first and final hole. unbuttoned.

half-conscious. throwing answers at an orange square
head spinning a wheel. spinning the wheel. rooting for a
promised escape. no destination in mind. no idea of route.

Catch

if this is a game then we have made it, unknowing,
to the final four. unlikely underdogs. spectators turned
to suspect sport. anti-athletes. out of shape beyond reason.

at season's height we fight for a limited audience. few dancers.
fewer cheers. down by 30 and our coach m.i.a. we, foolish, dribble.
each bounce-back brings a stranger. can't call us for traveling because

we ain't going nowhere. instead, we trade terrified looks. search
for the pass but no one stays open for long. even if we knew what to do
to pull this through we've got two other teams waiting, impatient, to take us out.

Consumptivitis

not enough anymore to endure banality
once. record. watch again over last week's
pepperoni pie. don't bother to reheat. wonder

would it be more efficient on tuesdays
to eat feces fresh. grow and harvest. feed,
water and feed again. or let it go to rot and store

for our next angry winter. hold tight toward spring.
promise on sun spots to interrupt reception. cue our few
cool, fresh water lakes. showcase lazy days spent quiet and afloat.

Juggling crystal balls

a rocket ship to the moon, boarding pass, first class seats,
packed bags, two feet to get up the stairs and still we stay planted.
every step requires lead lifting. the ground below and ahead invisible.

we must go. in this flight-taking lies our future. the moon is ours. with
its atmosphere we breathe. with its easy gravity we soar. survival of the journey
is no guarantee but standing here, frozen and inert on earth, secures quiet annihilation.

movement remains our only hope. every step requires lead lifting. can't see the ground?
wish it under every step. after all, it is a rocket ship. flying without a parachute seems silly,
but the tougher shot fits this thinning atmosphere. plus, as missiles, we are lethal. sure-fire. free.

When the saints went

what remained: barren stalks bowing heads
by the field-full. rusty air conditioners dripping
from warped windowsills. rock formations retaining roots.

hollowed out caves and dog stumps forced ragged, toothy grins.
all ablaze. a laser show shot hot through the tinny night. every husk
wore a well lit protrusion. every breath an asthmatic thrush more material

than the silence that surrounds each carcass now: voided prayer: cold
arthritic grating: remembering notions of breath. saints: offer a hand to a
wheezing shadow: wish for someone to hold before the sure, sudden twilight.

Waiting on the Reading

Many of my race have lived long without the touch of
these fine things which separate us from beasts. Things
I call my own now. Having served thirty-six years as needleman

for a family far more ape than we will ever be, I rode
the moonlight train to find my free. Up here it is colder than I like,
but the gentlemen admire my frock coats above all. I taught my son this trade

and hope this picture I made will help retrieve him. Come summer I leave
this coast for Philadelphia where I hear we of color can breathe yet more free.
Tonight I stitch. The breeze off the bay smells of aria. It is almost the season for cloaks.

Making black-eyed peas

Never mind the way the earth turned flat at the edge of where we lived;
this ritual remains. A midnight kiss, an overstocked pantry, a jovial welcome
at the front door for Mr. Jones, his arms laden with corn bread. This far north

the quaking aspens shimmy their leaves to the ground by October. But winds
these days stagger in low, west to east, anxious, drunk, stubborn, snatching stray
hard headed discs from sleeted branches to sweep through open windows for a last

dance with drizzled mustard dust, thick red peppers, green chiles and that extra pinch
of garlic. I count 365 pitch pitted pennies to each paper plate. I add a heap of surefire collards.
You pass your mother's ancient copper shakers. You ask: *How come you never spice up these peas?*

Body surfing

in. past the harbor. past the docks. beyond all ships. further still.
past pebbles and sand. after the washashores. beyond the point of seagulls.
along through the buoys and fisherfolk to where salty waters sink into song.

when you get to the edge of the sound, keep going. you'll have flexed
your fingers, stretched your toes, pulled your muscles loose. when you get to
skin call me. make sure you've scrubbed your hands, clipped your nails. tune in

to the beat. not only rhythm, but beat. when you get through skin hang left,
baby, call my name. what you seek rests just a little bit further on. hold your breath.
let me reach you. the rolling waves can be unsettling. fortunately, we've already eaten.

Remainder

not your koko taylor cds, or your good luck dancing socks.
not your crisp black belts, your ink pens or your red felt fedora.
your blue silk shirts were so soiled i used them as rags. never even

wanted your new jack swing or that thing you do with your eyes
that makes lies go down easy like honey. honey, you can have that
bottle of whiskey left under my kitchen sink. i think you need it more

than i do. leave the sponges, the mop and the lemon scented bleach.
leave the protein powder i save for my uphill days. i unstuck my salty laugh
from the birdlime bottomed basin. traded your negro league cards for new shoes.

Just in case

dance. rip sleeves from shirts. quick!
make up any excuse. strip down. don't
sit. get to the liquor store. go to the beach.

shhhh. laugh. somebody put on prince.
stroke hips. set to shake. sizzle. cook one
another. strike skin to skin so humidity drips

liquid lead: floor to ear to inside.
ride that c flat. if tomorrow we die tonight
let's fry some chicken. cut that watermelon up.

Dowsing crow

"Open sunflower!
Pry these lusty eyes from sleep.
Steep redolent blue."

Topographic shifts

your baby is healthy
they said
flawless
all her fingers
and toes
well…
they said

fingers and toes
at first breath labeled
wasteful *Look* they said
unswaddling blankets
with unmetered distance

twelve fingers
twelve toes
twelves ounces
of thick black hair
screamed from its roots
loud and intact only
for two days time

she must be
they said
corrected

*

This condition
is more common
than you'd think.

Body as altimetric waste
tucked into seeping bandages
scooped into waste bins with

the shaky precision of
an unlicensed torafugu.
Waste not; want not.

Problems of a different figure
must be addressed with urgency
before they find witness.

No one ask the body.
Its response cannot
possibly merit the wait.

*

How is it done—
remolding body into
image of body?

Scrubbed clean stranger
hands determined to know
best. Tell the mother

it will be easy. Get a bit
of string. Tie a tight bow
around each offending digit.

Pull. A bit of cooing
mixes well with an
ether-soaked rag.

When the finger stands
surrounded by string
shift the knot low to base-

level. Tight like shoelace.
Tighter still. Waste not, want
not. Quiet tuberous quaking.

Hold one end of string
between two clean fingers.
Two antiseptic unwasted fingers.

Secure other end between
two or three more. Hold
the baby. Keep the mother

away and sleeping.
Now rip. Root.
Cauterize.

*

Leaching toes proves
difficult. Feet arrive
stubborn, open to receive

their due. Feet fixed
as refugee children
at mother's skirt, toes
cling firm to fountainhead.

A task like mining mountains
once crystallized to bone.
Double up string then.

Find suture scissors boiled
and sharp. Tie at root
as before. Snip. Defeat

secular variations
at their earliest
appearance.

This condition
is more common
than you'd think.

Breakadawn

remember
can't walk

remember
every bone

wrenched
weeping

each
stinging
breath

every
raspy
moment

remember
can't sit or

stand or lie
absent agony

even in
stillness

*

remember drumming
fingers on nightstand
standing in for movement

remember smelling nothing
but mottled breath   stop
do it now   remember

*

breathe in deep

well
        deep

as   you

can

*

remember
each day
you swore
would be
your last

for instance
            today

you swore
your last

*

here you are
again   look
     look
          look

*

remember muscles
like pulled cheese
stiffened in the cold

remember hips
femurs clavicles
whistling
like bad brakes
and no money

*

remember smell?

not so much.

try to remember it!

*

sound
difficult to retain

remember instead
doctor after doctor
calling you   dirty
just dirty   shame
squeegees   cotton balls
ear drops   stabbing pain

think bloodied butcher paper
think morbid humiliation

*

remember
this body
has known pain
for years   years

remember slowly
now faster remember
from cell to senses
twilight to night

then choose again
before the breaking dawn

Reckoning song

what if i can shake it • and not break it what if i can shake it • and not break it what if i can shake it • and not break it what if i can shake it • and not break it what if i can shimmy • dance all of me • shimmy dance what if • i can shimmy dance • all of me • shimmy dance • i can shake and i can • shimmy i can • shake and i can • shimmy i can live with joy inside a poem in my hips • and i can bring all of me • to the dance floor too • and i don't have to • bend and hide my here • and here and here and • i don't have to choose • to not step or step • with fear • what if i can live • what if i can walk • what if i can dance • yes me too • dance what if my body can remember • that joy and make it • what if i can shake it • and not break it what if i can shake • it and not break it what if • i can shake it and not break it • what if i can shimmy dance all of me • shimmy dance what if i can shimmy • dance all of • me shimmy • dance • what • if • i • can •

Revelations

paper napkins
styrofoam plates
oilcloth supper tables

speckled wall mirrors
surfaces more festive
than natural or retained

twist top weeknights
jug wine smoked windows
coffee stained fingertips

in the yard
somewhere
there are goats

whining rakes adrift
red leaf mountains protect
bikes rusted and abandoned

screen doors
slammed
despite protest

hunters' moon
always too many nuts
crunching underfoot

*

generations
of river folk and
rain travelers make do

with what I have now
know how to coax
packing animals to sit

wait
share their load
bring mud bring clay

from place to place
we build we rest
we stay a while

five thousand aunties
love five uncles
teach a world of kin

tuck rifles and gin
into belts strapped
tight for flight but

even when we leave we don't
try to get rid of us—
good luck

*

nights I shudder
through memories
of drought

hands radiate heat
fusing half a world
into one night light

smooth jazz Sunday drives
where granaries used to sit
indict my loss of harmony

my own staccatoed tongue
lay like a silo
dormant

hung on greasy nails
next to old sheepskins
rusty hammers and spades

farm houses replaced
by big pharm and
big pharm mansions

aside from laughter
and pulse so little of
what is left seems useful

*

but baby
your cool melts
my moonpie heart

conjures dancers
who hop at this chance
to snap themselves open

slide flatfoot
across sawdust floors
grabbing skirts

to breast as in
prayer your river
meets my riverbend

turns more sharply
than I'm used to
but I don't mind

for once I don't mind
you lift your oilcloth
share your beermat stains

then bid me show you
mine so long hidden
crack my spine open

Carry her for me

this bitter toothless
mumbly old lady

she shouts at the government
via satellite   considers
sending very important
letters to the FCC and
McDonald's Corporation
the Vatican and whoever
is the boss of that nice man
down at the pet supply passes
free kibble when she's hungry

if she comes out back
and it ain't busy

hold close to chest my impulse
to horde stamps 'cause that lady
don't never have none
and this giant red frog
in my throat from all her
hollerin' and haranguin'
her smokin' too I'd imagine
I bump heads with her
in the shower sometimes

she hates to wash her hair

I throw away grocery bags
daily though I could swear I
never shop could swear instead
her bags grow in size and quantity
despite my antipathy
a magic drawer or
an old lady curse

be fruitless
multiply

Congress of crows

"Lay me on August
bluegrass and kiss me, you fool!
'Ware, you peck. I bite."

Mental healing in modern times

Wiser women than I have sought this healing.
Mind over body.   Faith over sight.
Believe I have received and I shall receive;
this healing principle operates in us all.

Mind over body.   Faith before proof.
My subconscious will heal the cut on my hand.
This healing principle operates in us all.
Only fools believe in things which hurt them.

My subconscious is healing the cut on my hand.
I imagine the end desired. I feel its reality.
I am not a fool who believes in things which hurt me.
I am in touch with the infinite healing presence within.

Imagine the end. Desire it. Feel it real.
I believe I have received. I have received
the infinite healing presence within. Wiser
women than me have sought this.

Simmering amaranth

I sodden indigo
I lavender scented
flowering
I flying
red feathered
golden breasted
grain fed
sneezing free
metallic air
shaking
frost from wing

dip
swim
dive indigo waves
wind fathoms
breast to breast
I color brown
no. 4975 I
steamed magenta
midnight earth
syrah spiced
southern hot
winter night
sodden

soiled
indigo
beat into
clay beat
into cotton
beat through
silken robes
I drape
I exquisite
I slide
I caress
nary chafe
you slip
you in
I over
moon

Here. Now.

Sticky. Held together by nothing
more than musk. Salty with well-worn need.
Undesired truths unheeded. Speaking in active
voice. Demanding to be taken. Bending
like a willow to the throaty demands of each other.

So, this is where we are. Dusty.
Smudge marks on our backs
from unwashed walls and window sills.
Lace torn from panties. Breasts freed
from narrow confines. Release, begged for
and given, echoed in the stolen corridor
where we struggle to catch our breath.

Here, I am balanced
on one spindly heel.
The other a spear poking
from your backside,
thrusting with you,
shaking as we shake,
secure that your desire
will keep me aloft.

Here is where we tear the screams
from our throats. This dampened corner
where I suck your scratchy throat
between my lips to contain your moans,

where I lower my heel to push
your strong thighs deeper.

Here, then, is where we land
and take off for flight after flight,
soar the ether like a swallow-tail
in search of a stream. This is where
what we speak becomes real,
where taste imagined materializes
into flavor savored with nothing to hide us
but the dim bulb in the corner and
the blanket of dust on our clothing.

We are here, after all, with work to do.
I shake out my skirts, best as I can,
and brush down your trouser legs.
The chorus demands we straighten up,
ascend the stairs into daylight once more.

Fix our glassy stares into focus. You have
what lingers on your lips. I hold tight
to what I've captured between my thighs.

Discussing the weather

White hot
flesh drips
perspiration pours
from burning temples to
spin into rivulets, catch and
gather where chest meets meaty
arms; where saline birth stretches to
thigh, steps to a traveling djembe beat.

Sun said:
Didn't want
to hurt you. But
you begged to be beaten,
gave me the whip and when
I raised these fiery arms all you
said was *Please* and *Thank you.* All
you did was stretch lengthwise for the burn.

I wipe
my hands before
speaking to you. Erase
evidence of my breathless
need. Suck down ice like a
pacifier. Attempt to stifle my
cries. They become louder, despite
attempts to cool my sweltering skin.

I've just returned
from the bathroom
sink. I bathed first in
what you left me. Fingers
became blistering tongue. Stifled
moans aroused anamnesis, devoured
rhapsodic flight to flood each corridor
with slick shimmyshake. Down the stairs

a cool breeze picked up
pace and quickened need.
Barometric shifts which left me
crushed then released enough steam
to coat each window pane with your name.
I wipe my hands before speaking. Rise fast as
my chest as mercury as skin burned and bled as boils
and hives long hidden erupt to meet your saintly rain.

Jesus gon' hear my song sho' nuff

— *for RB*

I fly on high notes
carried by footlights,
past black keys and white,
past pine frame and fine shoes
tapping on waves invisible
and clear as Sunday's
come to meeting bell.

I'm so glad I'm changed
every day I repay the favor.
O! But on this day made for nothing
less than salvation with a side of chicken
notes awaken me from yawning slumber.

It begins with a flutter at the pit of my stomach
rises to a warm sweet spot in my chest.
As I dress it begins to reach my throat
leak out in bits of cry—

      tickling over tongue
      whistling through teeth
      rolling over lips
      formed full for praise
      secure that my love
      rides crescendo.

When I reach the house where my love resides
my sisters have to hold me down or I'm gone.
Only the rafters and his lifeblood kiss
can keep me from glory on days like this.

I can get through the night alone

because I smell you on the wind;
because your musk seeps in over

husky perfume, through the lotion
on my thighs. The tang of you leaks

from the air conditioner, blows through
my hair causes leaves in Central Park to

sing. You breeze by me on the corner
carried on a wave of exhaust. You rise

above the fetid subway, blow over walking
dogs and their run-behind people. Your aroma

beats through the streets muting alpine trees
as they dangle from mirrors stuck in the past.

I inhale you when I close my eyes before
the incense in my living room, or the candle

by my bed. I can rest just this once tonight
because you seep in on the wind —

a tincture dying each breath blue.

On summer evenings

When I do
I picture you
filleted and grilled

a dusting of olive
oil peeled ginger
and leeks. Seasons.

I look at you
see skin and char
smoldering scars

as script. Constellations
shimmer and smoke. My love,
bid me singe with you. I'll sing.

Crow meditation

"Dip fevered neck. Plant
split-lipped calm. Spit wonder. Smile.
Starve dark fright. Be light."

Climate change

Springtime is at hand. When will you ever bloom if not here and now?

— *Angelus Silesius*

the sun rose noontime   like somebody had cussed his mama
sun had a bone to pick   a score to settle   and had come on up
to collect   late as a birthright   argument on lip   came   up
blazing steel mill style   wasn't nothing to do   but melt

pour through cotton   pour through silk   pour through linen
seep salt and funk   through every fiber   no   point trying
not to move   no   way   out

run if you want to   but the hill is steep   might be i didn't need
that eighth cigarette   chest full and drum hide tight   sun
beating on down   down   down   down   my cat died last month

or maybe it was the month before   i should remember   i held her
after paying good money to have her killed   good money

plus interest   to have my sweet baby put down   afterward
every homecoming met silence   no one waiting   no one caring
whether I was home or not   no one pissed about days and nights
when no one crossed the threshold bearing fresh food and a clean plate
even though they promised   fucking poets   not worth a damn

now she's dead   cancer   nothing i can do but hold
head up to madness   life and death   circumspect

*

i can't quit smoking.

that's a lie.   i just won't do it.

that's a lie.

i keep putting them down   i keep picking them up   put them down
pick them up   why do i not just leave it   i do   leave   this   breath
leave these teeth   leave this tongue   leave these lips   leave these fingers
leave   leave   leave   leave   this   concentration   witness:

i refuse to sustain an ongoing focus on what i am supposed to be doing
                              that's a lie
what i should do   why i should do it   i'll never know   that's a lie
i know   i just don't want to   leave it   i can't think

about it   leave it   it's all madness   madness   madness and
i had a near death experience the other day in the botanical gardens.
listen   i'm going to need you to care about this   because
i care about this   i need you with me   ready?
                                                                          care:

*

walking through lavender   cilantro
and scallions   running my fingers
over blooming poppies   plucking
mint leaves   from a labyrinth path
and popping them   under my tongue
to clear   the taste

fresh rosemary   northwestern sage
mesmerized by quaking aspens   quaking
in a soft breeze   too soft to penetrate
this heat   leave this sun

and the care   breathtaking   tender loving
care with which each shrub   each flower
each tree   each sprout is planted
and placarded   and protected

and   the   quaking   of   the   quaking   aspens
in the breeze   and   i'm   walking
lost   from   my   party

see a sudden goose   gander   goose
and gander and goslings a whole damned
goose family   walking ahead through
gardens to a radiant   rippling pond

*

whaddamigonnado?

i wanna sit by the pond   sit on the bench
by the pond and watch   gander   goose
goose babies   all that   so i walk closer

closer and gander starts gathering   family to pond
flapping his wings and   guiding goose and gosling
and gosling and gosling   one after another to
water   turning at me   hissing

every few steps   turning back at me and hissing
like a dead angry cat   and i'm walking
through the grass   sandals dodging gargantuan
goose shit   all the way   getting closer

closer to the bench   closer to the water
closer to gander   and damn
if this bird doesn't get his girl and his babies in the
water and come after me   damn if i didn't
just about get to the bench   just about sit
a few hundred duly dodged bombs   behind me

when this hissing gigant-a-bird comes squawking
charging and yeah   i screamed   what the hell
it was a flight monster   mad about his babies
i screamed and screamed   and ran

ran   ran   ran

caught   clowned   by my two-legged family
who right on time   decide to materialize
witness my attempted murder   seize upon wing
and claw and aural attack and laugh   still care?

madness   leave it

*

walking home
sun sports boxing gloves

dances light footed
heavy fisted

headed south ground
becomes cracked

spread   open
used and left

air gives warning
alerts nose before eyes

smell cinnamon sunlight
smell cayenne floccus

smell sticky musk before
it dissipates raw and abused

the year has been long
i must find grounding

glue to hold me steady
through this steadfast storm

*

through it all I require
your presence

Agó?!

and your
care

Amé!

even when there is
somewhere to think

Agó!?

even then there is
nowhere to think

Amé!

madness   pissy sun
madness   scurrying fowl
madness   teeming self
madness   flesh eating wind

madness   carrying bitters and sours
                        and not a damned thing
                            to mix them with

madness   this scorched thirst
        burning me closer to death

leave it   it returns

not the rays not the breeze
which cools them

not the gardens nor the streets
which beat them down and up

not the quaking trees
nor my quivering knees

can do this alone so I'm going to
need you to go ahead and care

(*agó?*) are you here?
(*amé*) good.
ready? care.

Getting strong

Demons be gone!
So too the siren's song
Let there be breath and chosen memory.
Forgiveness and forgiveness.

Joy!
A little ha ha and
some wild guffaw.
Fresh corn and apples.
Hot baked good things
savored slowly with
all the time in the world —
we've got all the time
in the world.

Yes!
We are lifting, curling,
raising muscles and flesh,
expelling anger and fear
with each out breath in sets
of twelve and fifteen and twenty
and sometimes we stack weight heavy
wear agony on our snotty sleeves
but not every day.

Not every day will feel this way:
walking through molten air

and burning man   burning
so hot we want a shot of anything
that promises to cool us down.

Demons and sirens are liars
of the most unscrupulous kind.
Not simple-minded hustlers
trying to win a wary dime but cold-
hearted killers who'll cover you in lime
build a house on your bones
and sell it to your left-behinds
at ten percent over market.

Promise we won't listen
to their songs. Promise
we'll forgive ourselves
for days we sit woofer
to ear weeping and pounding.
Promise we'll try not to kick
our bruised and swollen ankles
too hard   let in a little joy
a bit of ha ha and some wild guffaw
and remember that not every day will
feel this way.
Promise.

Hoof & Jive

In my ear an old cassette
Is set to run to the end
flip and play again. Incessant loop.
Worthless canto suffused with six-part harmony.
Scratched recording picked up years ago in a dusty bin.
Without abatement it hums. Flip and repeat. Steady rock
it sings like a tree planted by the water. I shall not be moved.

I should toss it. This song is not mine. Clammy midnight
congregations sway to a more familiar rhyme. We children
know it note by note by heart. I shuffle toward the rumble
brushing shoulder to shoulder with kin. We steady rock
four-by-four. We dervish desperate transformation. We creep
tender. We fall to floor. Hush and scream. Hoof and jive. Jump up.
Stand ground. Howl. Bay. Stand still. Stay right there. Listen. Bend
and release like a tree. Planted by the water I shall not be moved.

Lean back and swing. Over. Andante. Andante. Share redemption with any
old thing. Moan. Shout to windows. Tilt head up. Damn riverbed cheeks. Flip.
Repeat. Toss headphones. Toss shoes. Stomp over spilt Dixie cups. Let speakers
sweep tidy curls to source. Wind down. Start again. Force eyes wide. Unshutter.
Catch high notes at tongue tip. Open. Now. Open wider. Don't let go. Stay
planted like a tree by the water. Don't. Move.

Dance at the height of the sun

we scarin' water
to fall from the sky.

singing the sound
of mud at our feet.

shimmy shakin' fruit to flip
step from heavy branches

to growing baby bellies.
we makin' them babies

scream, man; howl their laughter
as fowl splits the spits.

Gospel

wind in fire
candles on altar
walk through temple   sing
stir fingers through holy water
pull dampness through hair
over temples   loosen
plump curls   dance with holy
raindrops   breathe

dance with fire
sway to altar candles
one two three
hundred prayers
for the living
for the dead
for those yet waiting
to enter

how many brides
have toed this path
pinching shoes to
keep them upright
father arm propulsion
through cool ceramic echoes

I slip on rose petals
I dance with fire

I sing high on holy water
I anoint with sensuous oils

make me a holy chamber
and I'll make you whole

dance with water
dance with fire
dance with lemonscent
as it wafts from pews

how many bodies have left this way
carried off with a last hipshake
on the shoulders of friends nephews
officiants trembling with the weight
of their task

dance with the pulpits
holding the beat of the fist
dance with the sun
streaming through colored glass
dance with earthen walls
dance with iron lung skies

I'll stretch my arms heavenward
push through painted ceilings
harden fingertips to punch through
wood and spackle and frothy insulation

I'll stretch a hole wide as a thousand stars
so when children shift their eyes
heavenward in distraction
they may still receive the word

the word says
we are holy
the stars will agree
that what we are
is holier yet
than the whole
of the world

Hugin & Munin disrobe in the locker room

Chiiiiiiiile!
Did you see that shit
sparkle brighter than full
moon's midnight and northern lights?

Epiphany!
That's what I'm'a call her
after my baby's mama.

Did you see that aft?
Trees I could nest in forever.
At least 'til sundown when
trouble gets undressed.

Chiiiiiiiile!
I heard that
girl with the doorknocker earrings
gives it up lovely.

I speck I might have to
check it out next time we go
round the west side

's only rumor though.
Bossman rumor and he'll nail
any old cow anyhow.
Chiiiiiiiiiiiile.

< stretch >

Hurry up and get ready.
It's roundabout wine-thirty and I
got tail to shake and sense to make.
That route like'ta wore me out. Then
singing them stories. Singing him songs.

Not a moment to think.
Remember
what that ol' tree said
to him god: *darkness behind you*
she said: *daylight has come*.

Flyin' round this old bucket
of neckbone, riverblood and
stinking rotten teeth does fuck
for fine feathers. I need a
bath. Some after work love.

Rest
these brokedown wings
on tender pulp.
Come morning
it's time, again, to fly.

Notes

The epigram, by Lebanese poet Vénus Khoury-Ghata, appears in the poem "The Seven Honeysuckle Sprigs of Wisdom," from the collection *Here There Was Once a Country*, translated into English by Marilyn Hacker.

In Norse mythology, Hugin and Munin (loosely translated: "thought" and "memory") are raven messengers of Odin, highest god in the pantheon and benefactor of inspiration to worthy poets. Each dawn Odin, having traded his eye for wisdom, sends forth his twin ravens to travel the war-torn world, return to perch on his shoulders and report all they have seen and heard. In *Gospel*, Hugin and Munin are represented both as a phantasmagoric chorus of crows in "Hugin & Munin speak the scene," "Dowsing crow," "Congress of crows" and "Crow meditation." Here they sit perched to carry the reader into and through each movement. They reprise as fully embodied, overworked, crotchety old black folk in the final poem, "Hugin & Munin disrobe in the locker room." Raven to crow, phantasm to embodiment, readers are invited to carry many mythological manifestations of our messengers across oceans, across land and into the spirit of each. They are bad mothershutyomouths. We listen. We heed. We ignore. We do each at our peril and toward our expansion. Know this: they know this.

"Mental Healing in Modern Times" is based on text found in *The Power of Your Subconscious Mind*, by Dr. Joseph Murphy (rev. by Dr. Ian McMahan).

The opening line of "Making black-eyed peas" was taken with the poet's permission from the poem, "The Shaw Brothers," by Afaa Michael Weaver. His beautiful poem appears in *American Poetry Now: Pitt Poetry Series Anthology* (Ed Ochester, ed., University of Pittsburgh Press, 2007).

"Climate change" features the phrases *Agó* and *Amé*, which refer to an Akan (Ghanaian) call and response discourse used to gain the focus of participants or audience; esp. teacher to student. *Agó:* "I need your attention, I have something important to share with you." *Amé:* "You have my attention, I am silently awaiting your words."

About the author

Samiya Bashir is the author of *Gospel* and *Where the Apple Falls*, a finalist for the 2005 Lambda Literary Award. Bashir is editor of *Best Black Women's Erotica 2* and co-editor of *Role Call: A Generational Anthology of Social & Political Black Literature & Art*. She has published three chapbook poetry collections: *Teasing Crow, Wearing Shorts on the First Day of Spring,* and *American Visa*. Bashir is a founding organizer of Fire & Ink, a writers festival for LGBT writers of African descent, and is an alumni fellow of Cave Canem. She has recently served as Writer in Residence at Soul Mountain, as James Cody Scholar for the James Dick Foundation for the Arts, and as Artist in Residence with The Austin Project. Her poetry, stories, articles, essays and editorial work have been widely published. Find out more @ samiyabashir.com.

Other books by RedBone Press

does your mama know? An Anthology of Black Lesbian Coming Out Stories (revised edition), ed. by Lisa C. Moore (ISBN 0-9786251-6-1) / $19.95

the bull-jean stories, by Sharon Bridgforth (ISBN 0-9656659-1-7) / $12.00

the bull-jean stories (Audio CD), by Sharon Bridgforth (ISBN 0-9656659-2-5) / $12.99

last rights, by Marvin K. White (ISBN 0-9656659-4-1) / $14.00

nothin' ugly fly, by Marvin K. White (ISBN 0-9656659-5-X) / $14.00

love conjure/blues, by Sharon Bridgforth (ISBN 0-9656659-6-8) / $14.00

Where the Apple Falls, by Samiya Bashir (ISBN 0-9656659-7-6) / $14.00

Spirited: Affirming the Soul and Black Gay/Lesbian Identity, ed. by G. Winston James and Lisa C. Moore (ISBN 0-9656659-3-3) / $16.95

Blood Beats: Vol. 1 / demos, remixes & extended versions, by Ernest Hardy (ISBN 0-9656659-8-4) / $19.95

Erzulie's Skirt, by Ana-Maurine Lara (ISBN 0-9786251-0-2) / $15.00

Voices Rising: Celebrating 20 Years of Black Lesbian, Gay, Bisexual and Transgender Writing, ed. by G. Winston James and Other Countries (ISBN 0-9786251-3-7) / $25.00

Carry the Word: A Bibliography of Black LGBTQ Books, compiled by Steven G. Fullwood, Reginald Harris and Lisa C. Moore (ISBN 0-9786251-4-5) / $16.95

Blood Beats: Vol. 2 / the bootleg joints, by Ernest Hardy (ISBN 0-9656659-9-2) / $19.95

In the Life: A Black Gay Anthology, ed. by Joseph Beam (ISBN 0-9786251-2-9) / $17.00

Brother to Brother: New Writings by Black Gay Men, ed. by Essex Hemphill (ISBN 0-9786251-1-0) / $17.00

You can buy RedBone Press titles at your local independent bookseller, or order directly from RedBone Press, P.O. Box 15571, Washington, DC 20003). Add $2.50 per book for shipping.